Praise for William Sheldon:

"Bill Sheldon's *Deadman* is like nothing you've read before, yet it speaks to universal quandaries and possibilities present in wandering the mazes of our lives where "Purpose is assured only in the ground." This collection is both a mythical journey of Deadman rolling and pushing himself from the grave to walk the world of the living where he lies down on building sites of big box stores, writes songs on popsicle wrappers, and even does a stint in a sideshow. But this is also a whimsical, bittersweet, witty, and poignant meditation on the gig of being human. "What is rendered/ is the truest blues," Sheldon writes of the music *Deadman* eventually creates and of the poetry altogether, which sidle up to the music of mortality. *Deadman* shows us, through Sheldon's succinct and brilliant language, where and who we are and might be, while reminding us to "Enjoy/ the river rolling on your right,/ the sunshine on this day under a sky/ so large it seems a question.""

~ Caryn Mirriam-Goldberg, 2009-13 Kansas Poet Laureate and author of *How Time Moves: New & Selected Poems*

"Considering the fact that *Deadman* is about a dead man, it shouldn't be so relatable. But it is, extremely. Unapologetically dark, hilariously funny, with the memory of TS Eliot buzzing throughout, *Deadman* is the very definition of haunting."

-Zara Lisbon, author of *Baby's First Apocalypse*

"Who is Deadman? *Deadman* is the mythos of our times, a comedy of errors, a hodge-podge of Shakespeare, Fitzgerald, Eliot, and other dead guys; and he's living in a contradiction as he "has had enough of being / the one true deadman walking." These poems trail through a narrative of what it means to be the living dead, not a zombie, but just trying to have a life for himself if others will let him. When you start following him, his world looks like ours or even yours, Dear Reader. He points us out in pop culture and Americana. Even trapped in the Anthropocene and exploring what this all means, even reincarnation, Deadman "wonders what good / the secrets of a past life would do / a Deadman anyway." Pick up the book and give a listen to the music of *Deadman*. You'll find his hook "the truest blues, / rivers roiling, and homes / never returned to."

-Dennis Etzel, Jr. author of *This Removed Utopia*

DEADMAN

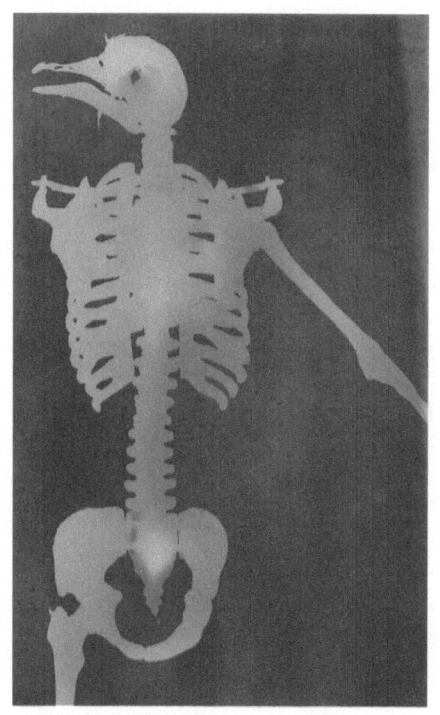

Poems by William Sheldon

Kansas City Spartan Press Missouri

Spartan Press
Kansas City, Missouri
spartanpresskc.com

Spartan Press

Copyright © William Sheldon, 2021
First Edition: 1 3 5 7 9 10 8 6 4 2
ISBN: 978-1-952411-46-5
LCCN: 2021930792

Author photo: Cindy Sheldon
All rights reserved. No part of this publication may be reproduced or transmitted in any form or by any means, electronic or mechanical, including photocopying, recording or by info retrieval system, without prior written permission from the author.

Acknowledgments:

I'd like to thank Brian Daldorph at Coal City Review for giving "Deadman #2" life. I'd also like to thank Harley Elliott and Steven Hind for their feedback on the early draft of the book.

Many thanks, especially, to Jason Ryberg and Spartan Press for walking Deadman into the world.

TABLE OF CONTENTS

In the Dirt

- #1 / 1
- #2 / 2
- #3 / 3
- #4 / 4
- #5 / 9
- #6 / 10
- #7 / 11
- #8 / 12
- #9 / 13
- #10 / 15
- #11 / 16
- #12 / 18
- #13 / 20
- #14 / 21
- #15 / 23
- #16 / 24

Doing Deadman Time

- #17 / 27
- #18 / 29
- #19 / 30
- #20 / 31
- #21 / 33
- #22 / 34
- #23 / 35
- #24 / 37
- #25 / 39

#26 / 41

#27 / 43

#28 / 45

#29 / 47

#30 / 48

#31 / 50

To Catch His Death

#32 / 55

#33 / 56

#34 / 58

#35 / 59

MetaDeadman: Notes and Two Poems

Notes / 63

a. / 66

b. / 67

To Cindy, who keeps me alive.

Life hurts a lot more than death.

-Jim Morrison

In the Dirt

1.

Deadman lays out a spread
for all his friends
who come, eyes or no,
to see him.
Those without,
shall nose him,
rich repast,
capon of dark mystery.
Such tales he could tell
of life forgotten,
remembered in his cells
and in those
who rode along.
He would be toastmaster
extraordinaire had dirt
not stopped his expression.
And he would speak of dreams,
if he could only wake.
Peace, Deadman, rest.
Take this morsel
of time, a strange stray
bays far away. Patience,
he will be here soon.

2.

Deadman, a little stiff, lies
almost awake
dreaming, in faint iambics,
of mermaids. Uncertain pressure
informs his sleep, dreams of deep
water, locked vaults, diminished
oxygen. Even the sky of his mind
oppresses. He wonders through his world
breaking down. If only he could wake,
but his eyes are weighted
as with copper,
and what his sleeping ears hear
troubles him. Sounds of crawling,
gnawing, and most troublesome
of all—a continuous seepage.
He is thankful for the mermaids,
and their song, even if, as he now
thinks, the songs are not for him.
Enough to lie here listening, his collar
high and tight. But then
a new sound, someone howling
through blankets of earth. And what
is that? Scratching?

3.

A dog whines at the door. Deadman
wonders: should he be the one
to open it, worries that doing
so breaks some protocol.
The attendant scratching
he finds grating,
here, supine, half-sleeping.
Surely someone will shoo the dog,
or welcome it. Why must he, stirred
from rich dreams (or so he senses them),
be the one? "Thus was it
ever," he thinks. "No, I'll not
be bothered, scratch and whine as you will.
I'll return to the gold and pink,
silver and green of dreams."
Then light
licks his face, snuffling
in his ears, and above all that hullaballoo,
he swears he hears birdsong.
As his eyes begin to adjust to this new
brightness, he says—says indeed—"Well,
this is unexpected."

4.

Deadman steps from the dirt.
In truth, steps is too dramatic.
He hitches to the side, rolls to his
forehead, pushes to his knees—
a great creaking—rises with waspy
jerks. Stands, stretches, looks
around, ignoring the raking light,
the nine call run of the Mocking Bird,
the leaves hollering full summer,
and is put off by the lack of witnesses.
Surely this great feat, pulled off
with no more intervention
than the pawing of a cur
must have witnesses.
Who will believe him? No fear,
my friend. Flies are gathering,
and vultures, your guidons. Green
now as Lazarus in your new situation,
you will grow tired of your celebrity.
Brush away the dirt. Bid your close
friends feed elsewhere. Look again.
It is the old world, not a next,
and it is deep, rich summer,
and you are   something.
Try out those walkers, old sport.
Spit the dirt from your words.
This is Christmas in July,
or Easter. What will you do

with the present? Your gait
is rusty and swings hiccuppingly
along, but you are moving
the right way (no
wrong) to town. Direction
will find you, or not.
You are like us now, Deadman.
Purpose is assured only in the ground.

This World Not the Next

5.

Deadman's first encounter
asks, "Do you need me
to call an ambulance?"
She adds, "You don't look so hot."
Deadman coughs dirt into his hand,
says, "Thank you, no."
His voice…
Her eyes mist.
"Can I make you dinner? Wash
your clothes? Bathe you? "
Perplexed, Deadman thanks her,
again, walks on. "Are you sure?"
she hollers at his stiff back.
"I can make you happy."
In this new world, material
but not real, what could make him
feel joy. In the distance, the sign,
though missing an I,
can still be deciphered:
MISS ON. Yes, Deadman thinks,
just what I need.

6.

Deadman lives, for lack of a better word,
in the downtown shelter
where they give him new clothes:
black suit and mostly white
shirt that will be his uniform.
He sleeps on a cot, eats soup, well crackers
mainly, drinks cheap rum with bums
in the alleys and never urinates
or defecates, some strange transubstantiation.
He doesn't need a job, but he looks.
This is not much fun, and he feels
a calling, or a desire for fame.
Like many, he feels his natural talent
(revivification) is being overlooked,
squandered. Notoriety,
like a satisfying piss,
eludes him. Every night,
as he lies on his cot to dream
(perhaps of mermaids), he thinks tomorrow,
I will find something. Danger!
Danger, Deadman! Already you have found hope.
The old guy, Güter, with the German accent,
and a tendency to preach, shambling
to his own bed, shakes wet hands
toward Deadman uttering a benediction:
"Piss be mit you." "Evidently,"
Deadman thinks, and then, "Tomorrow and..."

7.

Deadman walks when he can
face to the wind, which helps
some with the flies.
Vultures, circle overhead,
confused by his mobility.
They are nuisances,
impossible to arrive unannounced,
black surtout of flies
and a Mongol horde
of bald attendants. Women
love Deadman, who can say,
"I have come back to tell you all,"
and mean it, but he is arrested
time again by these hangers on,
mosca and voltore, set on him
by some bloat king to dog him
as he tries to make time.
Sometimes he thinks, "If only he ran
straight into a stiff breeze,
I might outdistance them,"
but that would be undignified, and his gait
is in disrepair. Thus, collar to his chin,
he keeps his neck stiff and strides on, star
and his entourage of parasites.

8.

Deadman goes swimming,
The county sheriff
casts a grappling hook
his way, where he performs
his float, hauling him to shore.
There is confusion
and the sheriff's half-hearted
apology: "I nearly died—
no offense—when you started
thrashing like that. Maybe
you ought not float. Keep moving.
It'll help with those flies. Y'all
have a good day. Oh, and sorry
for your loss." Deadman
towels off, thinks better
of working on his tan.

9.

Deadman rests in the waiting room
of the clinic where he will disappoint
doctors looking for signs of life
He looks at the cover
of *My Life With the Chimpanzees,*
a young chimp holding a young
Jane Goodall's thin right arm.
He fixes on her full right leg, flexed,
disappearing into her khaki shorts, her derriere
somewhere beyond the picture, her blond
hair, in a loose ponytail, swoops
off her high aristocrat's forehead, over half
a perfect shell of ear. Her patrician nose
and slightest overbite lead him
to believe he's discovered some secret
of his past. He cannot keep his eye
off the muscular leg, tan and shapely.
He would die, he thinks, with no sense
of irony, to be that chimp, frozen
like Keats' lovers.

                        Two days later,
he hears her, Jane Goodall, on NPR,
learns she is 80 or something, remembers
he is dead, or something like it,
hears a man say he saw a woman
with a walker at a Rolling Stones
concert, realizes that you earn your moss,
your wrinkles, that baby chimps grow old

and mean enough to rip your limbs off.
He likes the sound of Jane
Goodall's voice. She is talking extinction,
but she still sounds hopeful, happy
even. He would like to feel that way,
wonders how often she does, looks
one last time at the leg on the cover
of the book, wonders what good
the secrets of a past life would do
a Deadman anyway.

10.

At first, Deadman thought himself the one
who woke underground, a cumbersome
way to self-identify. Then came the flies,
and he thought to call himself Beelzebub,
but it seemed a limiting *nom de plume.*
And he knew "woke up" was euphemism.
So for a day he became The Dead Man
but soon grew tired of the article
imagining the extra work signing checks
or autographs, capitalizing the D and the M,
so like a pop star or a crime fighter
revised himself into a single word:

                                        Deadman.

Each day as he sets off, he cries,
in his dry voice, "Deadman walking here,"
chuckles, perambulates in his strange stride
so unlike Batman's or Shakira's.

11.

Deadman knows he is a character,
a word he pronounces accenting the second
syllable, like some itinerant actor in the 1800s,
playing the bard while his partner
picks pockets among Abilene's groundlings.
Deadman, himself a conman, says character
to be funny, or annoying; he's not sure which,
struggling as he is with motivation. His name,
all one word, he takes from a white faced
figure in red, remembered, he assumes,
from a comic book of youth,
and of course coming awake
to find himself within this play
he will play out (as if he has a choice)
once he finds his way into character,
a word he hears in his head
the way you and I say it.
He would like to be a crime fighter,
a dead cop sent back in search the earth
for his killer. Decent motivation.
But he cannot recall his own death.
Thus, he is a dead man walking: the street,
his dog, if he had one—his liberator,
with the muddy paws and friendly tongue,
long since run off. Perhaps he will buy a gag
leash, stiffened with wire, leading to an empty
collar so that one walks an invisible
pooch. "An effect so real, your friends will think

the dog is actually there." He wonders
who will get the joke. The wind
is gathering. He brushes at the flies around
his face, wishing it were his call
for make-up and that he knew what mood
his persona should suggest.

12.

Deadman does a stint in a sideshow,
becomes hard and cold,
in the metaphorical sense.
He makes the state fair circuit:
the rich smell of cowshit, horseshit,
pigshit, poultry-shit,
fried shit on a stick, AC/DC
blaring from the midway, and Deadman
talking to the fattest lady
he has ever seen, a "three-fer"
because she also sports a beard
and is billed as a mystic, believing
she can hear into the beyond.
Deadman feels for her and almost
makes up stories about being dead,
Instead, they critique the vintage
rock booming from the Tilt-
n-Hurl, as she calls it, and ignore
insults from the rubes, and calls
for Deadman to "do something,"
as if returning from the dead
lands were not enough.
The Bearded Madam Blavatsky
cannot stand on her own,
but she makes herself
erect, saying "Leave this man
alone. He has come back.
He knows what none of us

knows." Her gravity (almost
that of Pluto, Deadman thinks
unkindly) silences them.
"Tell us, Deadman," one woman
whispers. "Tell us
what you know." "You will

                              all die."

"No shit," a teenage boy
mutters. The woman,
like all but his friend beside him,
nearly faints at his voice, whispering
"Beautiful."

            "It will be black,"
he continues. "There is nothing
there. Worms and water
will have their ways
with you." There remains
only rapt silence,
until the fat lady whispers,
"That's not true." Deadman
looks to her (and not without pity),
then to the crowd, as if to say,
"Whom would you believe?"
They file past to see
the two-headed calf,
the other humbuggeries
they have paid way too much
to see. The next day, Deadman
is without a job.

13.

Deadman is a wonder to women,
not because he was dead and is now alive,
nor because of the rigor so evident
in his trousers. Well, these things too,
but it is his voice, more the sound
of mortality than money, say, but
there is something beyond
its whispered compulsion
that weakens their legs,
softens their loins.
He never pays for a drink
or lights his own cigarette,
even though no one but Deadman
seems to smoke much anymore.
Waitresses call him "Honey" and mean it
in ways they cannot comprehend.
He has only to say "Hello," or "May I
have some crackers," to order coffee,
and some barista is on her knees,
if only with her eyes. It is a power
he could use for evil, were
he aware. But he is lost in self-
absorption, in the question, "Am I
really alive?" So when the young
woman behind the counter
asks, "Is there anything else I can do
for you?" or "Room for cream?"
and Deadman replies, "Let's just fill it up,"
there is no end to the confusion.

14.

Deadman likes his coffee black.
Cream and sugar only hide the bitterness
that is his truth. Black coffee is a marvel.
Deadman has become dogmatic.
He wants coffee black as his suit, his mood,
as flies' eyes. He sneers at latte, at mooks
sugaring Americanos at Starbuck's, takes offense
at those saving room for cream
and begins to proselytize. His fly-
shrouded visage, his raiments
smelling of loam and the grave,
despite their newness: these things,
along with the barista calling "Deadman,"
should be signs and wonder, should
incite fear, at least awe. However,
ranting against condiments,
he seems only a bum, some
fundamentalist snake handler
unfathomably graced with groupies.
He should reveal; instead,
he chastises some poor mother,
on her way to daycare, denouncing
her choice of artificial sweetener,
calls the besuited businessman
"Sissy" for his frappe. (Deadman
would have an aneurism if he could.)
"Dilute not the essence of ambrosia,
of aphrodesia!" he pronounces,

and the young girls that follow like flies
squeal and swoon. "Pollute not the purity
of blackness, which is all, all, all!"
Best to leave when he's like this.

15.

Deadman takes to wearing a hoodie,
neither as political statement, nor
as nod to fashion, he simply enjoys
the view, a tunnel only of what faces him,
time as it should be,

                not as it is.

Deadman is "all about" moving forward
(toward what, he has no idea).
He feels he pulls a coach chock full
of drunken lords. The richest,
and drunkest, has thrown the driver
from the seat and taken up the reins.
Deadman hears the mad-drunk,
"Gee-up! Hyah!" feels the traces crack
across his back, and knows great comfort

                for the briefest moment.

Deadman takes no real comfort, no
pleasure in life, only pretends to. He knows
his hood is no set of blinkers, that no one,
no matter how mad, or drunk,
has steerage of his course.   He is alone.
Live alone. Die alone. (And then,
whatever Deadman's doing.)
Fold your hood back, Deadman.
The sun blazes away its certain
time. Water is cycling.
And a sparrow is flying, providence
free, toward you.

16.

Deadman walking, down the street,
flies swarming. Deadman
inattentive. Until the sparrow
from the blue meets his forehead.
An epiphany. He is not a murdered
cop's ghost, bent on holy vengeance,
not a prophet returned to tell us anything,
nor is he Hamlet, and this
penchant for black may be pretention
and worth rethinking. He is
John Doe, pedestrian,
struck by a furniture van, just someone
"not from around here," wallet lifted
while he lay dead, buried in a pauper's
grave, in a cardboard coffin, no one
to claim him, no one who knows
his name. But he does, though it no
longer matters. He was lonely then,
his apartment a box. Now he
has followers, and not just the flies
and circling birds, but real groupies,
women, who hang on him. Whom
he was can be put to rest. He
steps over the still sparrow. Now,
he thinks, is Deadman time.

Doing Deadman Time

17.

Deadman reveals himself
first to local news, laughs
as the anchor posits live
burial, ignoring the flies
that make filming difficult
and the general breakdown
of tissue, although sandy
soil has left Deadman
more mummy than worm-
eaten horror from EC Comics
or bloated floater dragged
from some river. He was dead,
is something else. Still,
his ribs imprison no heart.
What he is he cannot tell
any more than he can say
what it means that he is back,
than he can say if he is glad
or not, or what he will do
if the answer is "not."
Decapitated, say, will he walk
like Anne Boylyn's ghost,
head tucked underneath his arm?
It is a mystery he desires
not to face.
Not entirely happy here,
he is not ready to "die."
He is like you and I. "No,"

he says, looking
into the camera's lone eye,
"it's not live burial
you have to worry about.
It's staying dead
once you're in the ground."

18.

Talk shows would make Deadman Lazarus,
but the idea has no legs; he's nothing
to say. He speaks only briefly of the afterlife
His cells, he says, were aware of the "sounds"
of visitors. He places sounds in stiff finger quotes.
He says he was aware of the ludicrous
clump and hustle of the world above,
so like pedestrians on heavy glass
a world unaware of the real work
going on in the dirt. Even this
is a lie. Deadman remembers nothing
but perhaps the vaguest dreams
fading. He "woke" (no finger quotes) moments
before the dog's scratching and licking.
No one wants to hear that it was black
as ether, his rebirth the waking,
confused and in vague pain,
in some third world recovery room.
And no one wants to hear that yesterday
he saw that selfsame dog, the one
who dug him up, dead on the roadway,
and that the flies that had formed a canopy
between himself and the above world,
since he had hitched himself from the dirt,
left him for the dog and have not
returned. No longer do the indignant birds
circle overhead. Deadman, alone,
knows what a holograph feels.

19.

Deadman needs a job beyond
ex-sideshow freak on morning news.
Many things have been kept from him.
Waiting tables was out—always "flies
in my soup." Never urinating,
he cannot take, much less pass
a piss test. He feels himself falling
into uselessness when one station offers
him a part-time weather gig on grey days
where he will walk on set, umbrella
in hand, black bowler on his head to pronounce
Eeyore-like, "It's probably gonna rain."
He takes it "until something better comes along."
Decides one morning on a grotesque
(given his stiff gait) rendition
of "Singing in the Rain." Two bars in,
the anchor faints and wets herself.
The female producer yells, "I'll die for you!"
Calls light up the switchboard, (or would
if such things were not as dead as our hero):
young girls, middle-aged mid-level executives
striving to break glass ceilings, nurses
on the geriatric wards and their female patients,
all crazy over Deadman's voice. Day's end,
Deadman has an agent, a band, and a tour
lined up. Deadman has a job.

20.

Deadman's first gig is grotesque;
the audience frightens him, teenage
girls calling, "Deadman,
Deadman, let me die for you!"
He barely makes it through
the first song's first verse before
they swarm the stage,
honey bees keeping security
busy intercepting them, tackling
them, hauling them off, slung
over their shoulders (to copulate
with them later he learns, because
unable to have Deadman, or part
of his dark garments, these girls
want some sort of souvenir). At first,
he is appalled by the whole scene.
He senses his band's disapproval
of his prudishness. He could not
care less. They are studio hires.
His next tour he'll put together,
cats as hungry as he is, he thinks,
as he works his way to the final
verse, its crescendo. These guys
are history, and history, he knows,
is interchangeable.
                    The crowd
too is hungry, roaring,
screaming, "Let me die with you!"

And what should he make of that?
And suddenly he feels his deity.
And why not?
He makes his halting way
to the nearest SECURITY T-shirt
not busy tackling teen queens,
and above the hullabaloo,
shouts, "5th row, middle, yellow
halter top! Backstage passes!
She and her friends!"

21.

Deadman's first kiss—not counting the black
dog who dug him up and the sparrow
who flew into his forehead, or his mother
who parted the veil of flies and fainted,
then hugged him, planting the faintest peck
on his cheek—was not that satisfying.
The backstage groupie willing to do
anything, "die for him," "with him"
stuck her studded tongue
down his throat, and he felt nothing,
or, more precisely, nothingness.
And when she rode his perpetual vigor,
the transaction seemed more duty
than satisfaction. She, however, spread
the word like a flower, and Deadman was besieged
by a new swarm.

     He had hoped to taste life,
or at least amazement, as when the dog
and light licked his face. Instead, he felt only
his own mortality. He wishes
he'd have petted the dog, rather than
pushing it away (still feeling
the soft fur of its neck) or maybe
strangled it and pulled the dirt, like covers,
over both their heads. It has been that kind
of day. He curses a thought, newborn
and quickly choked down: "There is always
tomorrow." Deadman finds himself falling
into old, bad habits. Hope is a drug,
more addictive than meth.

22.

Deadman waits impatiently for the one,
half expecting her to wander
into one of his concerts
wearing a dress of green scales.
Standing in the front row, her mouth
will open to sing the water song he loves
but leaves others cold when he sings it.
Her voice will take him under,
draw him close like a light in fog
across a bay. She will sing the long
lullaby he would know again.
Deadman knows she will never
come, that his days are past
their best, but he decks his dream
with enough bright feathers to form a boa.
Instead, he looks down from the stage
to see some boy index and little fingers
raised, head-banging to the bass. Young
girl in a push-up bra, red as a heart,
shining through her white
T-shirt, "Deadman, I'll die for you,"
in black, tour dates on the back.
Deadman fears he'll live forever.

23.

Deadman needs no cucumber,
encumbered by tight leather pants
to impress his audience,
death is nonstop Viagra.
Perhaps that is what they mean
when they scream, "I'll die
with you," just the little death.
Now the flies have left, he looks
a little like an unwell David Bowie,
cheekbones without fat, higher
and sharper than seems
humanly feasible. Striking
in his tux, he is something beyond
heroin chic. He has tried
this new swarm, and while he
is every backstage girl's dream,
those trysts have left him cold.
He has bought a partner
from the back of a magazine,
nothing inflatable, something
latex and expensive, weighty
with lifelike hair, in the corner
of the dressing room. Sitting
in the cheap bra and thong
she came with, she looks almost
real. After concerts, he sits
beside her, sipping tequila,
eating crackers, patting her hand.

They are perfect together.
For what he spent he could be
pasha of an inflatable harem
in a bouncy castle, but he has
money and an accountant
to take care of it. Life after death's
been better to Deadman
than before.

He is waiting
for his girl. She will show
he is sure. Until then,
he has found someone more
his speed.

24.

No one could say Deadman has a good voice.
They turn his fans away the first day
tickets go on sale, within the first half hour.
Something in that voice, its deathless song,
(let's not say, "lifeless") draws them (let's not
say, "Like flies"). But the stuff he sings—Manilow,
Cuomo… The crowd is too young to know
and wouldn't listen to it to please their grandmas.
Deadman sings in a tux fronting an ex-punk
band, his band, playing low and slow
because his name lets you know the tempo. The band
knows it's a train wreck, tell Deadman the plugs
protect their ears. They eschew monitors. The crowd,
though, is enthralled, shackled
to his ghostly heart. And now that he has sung
his songs long enough, they no longer scream
"I want to die for you," all through the set,
only chant it at the end of each song. Deadman
doesn't care. The band gets drunk on better and better
whisky, the playing gets worse as the nights
and weeks walk on, The crowd doesn't care
Deadman is sanguine, no artistic
temperament here. The concerts are a ruse,
a disguise to cloak a quest in. So when the bass
player suggests, "Man, let's mix it up a little,
really confuse 'em, throw them a song
from The Boomtown Rats," Deadman flashes
his rictus grin, says, "Sure, whatever

you cats think best." And the bassman knows
the music is going to take a turn for the better.
The music means nothing to Deadman,
working on his holy ghost building.

25.

Deadman wishes he could play guitar
or even the lowly bass, but his fingers
feel too stiffly the strings. Nothing
transpires. No sense flows up
or down his arm, so even when he hits
the note, it's dross. He can only sing,
if you wish to call it that, his voice
the quality of stone decaying,
bacteria changing a possum into
something new. That's what draws
the crowds, sounds of real immortality.
But in what pass for his dreams,
Deadman plays like Hendrix, Atkins,
Van Halen, Knopfler (without
the headband, Deadman's forehead
Richards' skull ring). He exercises
his fingers with the gripper he ordered
from the back of a magazine,
envisions his digits moving, seeing,
feeling, hearing, touching the strings
like Townsend. (Deadman has
smashed a few guitars, never his,
buying his bandmates better ones.)
The lines, though, are mostly down,
his fingers' movements as strange
as his legs'. At first he thought this
a boon, that he'd play with same unholy
call to prayer his voice possessed.

But no. His fingers move like a spider
from which some cruel boy
has pulled half the legs
to turn it loose into the world.
Deadman, his humor a little dark,
laughs at his simile, takes another
swig from the bottle the guitarist
has handed him, notices the label
on the bottle's neck has slid
a little off like sloughing skin,
starts to laugh again, then sees
the bottleneck and realizes
the answer to his dilemma is only
a few swallows away.

26.

Deadman plays a killer slide,
the old Gibson tuned to open D,
notes low like the hole
he crawled from. He plays it old
style, the whole bottle clenched
in his talon of a hand, the bottle's
neck sliding up and down the guitar's
never touching the frets, the sound
harsh and strange. His voice
makes Howlin' Wolf's sound like
an angel, and his guitar makes Johnson's
sound like a harp. At his first concert
with the slide, a girl dies, just dies.
"Music So Bad It Kills!"
the papers scream, until her friend
reveals her last words: "Love him."
They start to die at every concert,
a fad. Young girls overrun a police
barricade in Cleveland set up to stop
the concert from happening, injuring
five cops. The city burghers,
who cancelled it beg Deadman
to perform before the Bacchanalia
runs entirely amok. Before he hits
the stage, a young man selling $6
hot dogs is pulled over the counter
and rent limbs from torso. The girls
set up a plaintive wail as Deadman

hits his first chord, presents
the crowd his rictus grin. Twenty-one
die that night, a new record.
Deadman is neutral
in response, simply glad
he's found a way to play guitar.
He knows the French are correct:
You have to sacrifice, suffer even,
for beauty.

27.

Deadman loves Townes Van Zandt
plays "Black Crow Blues" repetitively
and laughs. It is hard to tell
if he is being rueful. Soon he plays
a slide version. It does not go well.
He breaks up laughing at every concert.
Most times the crowd, an amoeba,
does not get it, senses he is laughing
at it, and perhaps he is. The mob, in turn,
turns on him. At a concert in Oklahoma
City, the crowd yells, "Why don't you
just die" at the end of every song
and then continuously. At Madison
Square Garden, simply "Die, bitch!"
When it starts throwing pennies
heated with cigarette lighters,
at Deadman's and the band's
eyes, the guitarist drags the frontman
offstage as Deadma gives the audience a boney
finger. The riot that follows does enormous
damage, but the only death
is unrelated, a drunk father picking up
his son and his date runs over two
boys huddled in the parking lot
lighting a joint. It is nearly the end
of Deadman's career, but then his label,
using old concert footage and overdubs,
puts out a video: "I'd Die 4 U
(If I Only Cud)." It becomes a rotation

unto itself. Soon all the kids wear
rubber bracelets with the initials
WWDMD. Deadman tries to hang
himself. It is embarrassing. He is found
by his maid who cuts him down
and immediately resigns,
A tabloid pays well for her story.
She becomes famous
for a coffee break, makes a little money,
not as much as she needs, or at least
as she wants, then disappears forever
from our tale. Deadman, to his chagrin,
becomes a messiah. "He tried to die
for you!" touts one paper. The Church
of Deadman springs up in every major
city. Suddenly he has a new gig, and less
chagrin. He can preach his gospel of black.
In Seattle, a man ordering a Caramel
Frappuccino is stoned to death. Deadman
loses what little sense of himself
he has left.

28.

The Church of Deadman is a bad idea
(even its acronym) from the start.
Deadman, if not crazy, has gone a bit off.
News shows ask, "What kind of church
has, as its first, commandment something so arbitrary
as 'Thou shalt drink thy coffee black'"?
This time, Deadman knows the answer.

        Still, Deadman offers no
consistency. Commandment number two:
"Thou shalt play an instrument," serves
of course as excuse for Deadman's singing.
Spoons and kazoos abound, and bad strumming
like Sunday in Guitar Center.
His bandmates show up once, a courtesy, laugh
uproariously on live television, are fired
and excommunicated.
The label rehires them almost as fast,
but they are banned from services
forever. Fine by them. Still,
a certain stiffness remains
between them and their lead singer.

COD is doomed to fail. Deadman
has no sermon on his rejuvenation,
nothing occult. He just wants everyone
to think like him. As a minister,
his motivation is correct but lacks
proper mysticism. People lose interest.

Some folk like cream and sugar,
and some have no rhythm.
Others in the church
are more successful. Soon
his teachings are supplanted. A rival
rises with his own agenda,
(of no matter here). Deadman
is the thin white face of the church,
but the power belongs to the rival,
whose visage is that of a bloated toad,
his voice sonorous as Orson Wells,
his message all poison Kool-aid.
He will eventually be blamed
for more deaths than Deadman (no
tale for now). Enough to know
that soon COD and Deadman
arrive in court battling for the use
of his name. The ruling favors
Deadman but the trial exacts a toll.
(Still, he laughs when people tell him
he looks pale.) He cuts the cord
with the church he inadvertently founded
(now called The Church of the Walking
Deadman With Signs Presenting—no
acronym) and goes back on the road.

29.

Deadman writes his first song,
music and lyrics.
It is of water passing
through and by as one lies
alone embraced by soil.
It is a train song, a lover leaving
song, that the living do not get,
though they love his voice,
and the band plays like hell.
It is a dilemma.
                He is flattered
by their adulation.
But he desires deeper
connection, an old story,
one without a happy ending,
Endings seem irrelevant
to Deadman. "All I can do,"
he thinks, "is write," regarding
right away how trite that sounds.
Finally, he has come to understand.
He writes another song about water,
trying to get it right.

30.

Deadman walking
a gravel bar by the river
discreetly wondering
about throwing himself in,
comes upon the perfect
bottle for a slide—
green glass, a little longer
than his middle finger,
raised letters:
"Mrs. Winslow's Soothing Syrup."
Without wondering why,
he bites a little below
the bottle's neck,
spins it in his mouth,
spits out the bottle's neck,
a neat trick,
one he wishes he'd have had
at the freak show.
It now fits perfectly
his long ring finger.
No more taloned grip
on a whole bottle.
He'll throw himself in
tomorrow, drown
or find the delta.
Today, he wants to know
Mrs. Winslow.
Google and the lead guitarist
phone-summon her ghost:
teething drops from the late

1800s, their main ingredient,
morphine, a favorite
of soldiers home
from the Civil War.
"Baby Killer," it was called.
One ad shows a mother
in white gown
touching her baby's teeth,
like God touching Adam
in Michelangelo's
mediocre ceiling.
Deadman could sleep,
really sleep. Maybe
morphine, or heroin,
(also found in teething drops
his guitarist says). The image
of his living mother is less
clear than that of Mrs. Winslow.
Adam though he is, he knows
no god. No one
told him "get up
and walk," to throw off
the clothes of the grave.
Even the dog who raised him
is dead. He plays
the slide on the Gibson
hollow-body.
What is rendered
is the truest blues,
rivers roiling, and homes
never returned to.

31.

Deadman writes the perfect song
on a popsicle wrapper tumbled
down the street at just the moment
of his inspiration. The song
captures everything he knows,
feels about being alive
                          after being dead.
It is a perfect blues. He folds
the sticky wrapper, carries it
in his palm, a kind of grail, home
to the Fender Nocaster
and the green glass slide.
Finger in the slide, the slide
just touching the strings, the tubes
in the tweed Champ
warming, his head
in a minor key, Deadman knows
this is going to be good.
                          He opens his mouth
at the amplifier's hum and begins
to bawl. There are no tears,
just dry, wracking sobs. It is hours
before they subside. He has leaned
too close to the amp.
The feedback calls him back.
He switches it off, racks
the ancient Fender.
By the last light of the day, filtered

through the blinds, he pulls a small
framed photo off the studio wall,
removes the picture of himself
and the original Deadman Band,
replaces it with the wrapper, rehangs
the frame on the wall. The world
will have to wait.

To Catch His Death

32.

Rain is falling. Deadman lies
on the ground of a construction site
of a new big box store. The earth
is soft, running to mud, beginning
to ooze. He is tired, of everything, really:
girls dying for him because they cannot
be with him, his "career," the same
inane questions—not, "What
is like being dead?" which is,
of course, the only question, but rather,
"What is it like being alive again?"
If he is alive,
the answer is: the same. Your problems
are Deadman's problems. Hence the mud.
He wants to return to the seep
and gnaw, that sort of breakdown,
not this one he is suffering.
He has covered himself
completely now, the only child
on a rain-scalded beach.
Two hours later, tired of holding
still, he comes unburied yet again,
stands, curses the universe
and does not die, makes his strange way
home, where the new maid admonishes him
that he'll catch his death.

33.

Deadman truly is the thin
white duke. All comment
on his high cheekbones,
on his skeletality.
He is blamed for a new
dieting fad, life-taking
anorexia, Post-mortem Chic.
He has neither to play
or sing and girls and boys
die for him. He is perplexed
by death threats he receives
from anguished parents.
So much of this new "life"
confuses him. He
has become the big "get"
for every party from NY
to LA. When he shows
up, he rarely makes it
to crackers at the food table
for all the hangers on.
Sometimes he misses
the flies, who at least
made sense. He drinks
expensive champagne,
which never passes
wine to water.
Women kiss his cold
cheek, compare it

to the flip side of pillows.
None of it matters
to Deadman, who only
wants another cracker
and to discover his
raison d'etre, adrift
on this river, a raft
without steerage,
a Duke without a Prince.
A young girl presses
her face against
the Deadman's
limo, a shadow moving
through a gate
somewhere in the hills
above the Pacific.
"I would die for you!"
she mouths through
the glass. "So would I,"
Deadman says to no one,
"If I knew how."

34.

Deadman has had enough of being
the one true deadman walking.
Even his art will not sustain.
Tired of his own voice, and finally
even of the slide moving up the strings,
Deadman would have an end to it.
Always before, that bobber, hope,
had popped back up, and Deadman
had found reason to move on. Now,
though, is enough. A big fish
pulls the bobber. It will not rise.
Deadman has found real purpose:
how to make an end? Peace,
Deadman, old friend. Enjoy
the river rolling on your right,
the sunshine on this day under a sky
so large it seems a question. Those
who can help are on their way.
Together they are not afraid,
and all of them are hungry.

35.

Deadman ends ignobly, some would say,
not so Deadman. Reborn of canine attention,
what better way to leave than at the teeth
of a pack of feral strays, acting upon our basest
need. Slim pickings, Deadman thinks, and laughs,
coming undone, feeling little of what we
would call pain, but, surprisingly, a bit of longing
for things not done. For the curs, it is cotton candy,
dry morsels disappearing almost the instant
they enter their mouths, even his bones
unsatisfactory, until all that remains
is laughter in the empty sky
as they stalk for shadows, like us
unsated by repast.

MetaDeadman:

Notes and Two Poems

Notes:

1. Line 6, "shall nose him," William Shakespeare, *Hamlet*, IV, iii, 33.

2. 3, "faint iambics," Edgar Lee Masters, "Petit the Poet," *Spoon River Anthology*. MacMillan, 1916. Line 3.

18, "they do not sing to him, etc." T.S. Eliot. "The Love Song of J. Alfred Prufrock." *Collected Poems: 1909-1962*. Line 125.

5. 15-16, "material without being real," F. Scott Fitzgerald. *The Great Gatsby*, Scribner, 1925. p. 161.

6. 19-20, "Danger! / Danger…" *Lost in Space* (1960's television series).

7. 15, "mosca and voltore," see Ben Jonson's *Volpone*.

16, "bloat king," *Hamlet*, III, iv, 185.

22, "collar to chin," "Prufrock," 42.

11. 11, "comic book of his youth," DC Comics introduced the character Deadman in *Strange Adventures* #205.

13. 8, "its whispered compulsion," *Gatsby*, p. 9.Notes, p. 64:

15. 21, "steerage of his course," Shakespeare, *Romeo and Juliet*, I, iv, 113.

    27-28, "providence free," *Hamlet*, V, ii, 219.

16. 5-6, "murdered / cop's ghost," *Strange Adventures* #205.

17. 10-11, "EC Comics / or bloated floater," see, for instance, EC's *The Vault of Horror* #15 or *Tales from the Crypt* # 24.

18. 1, "would make Deadman Lazarus," see John 11:1-44 and Luke 16:19-31, *KJV* for the two Lazarus stories.

    26, "indignant birds," William Butler Yeats. "*The Second Coming.*" *Selected Poems and Two Plays of William Butler Yeats*, Collier, 1962. Line 17.

19. 12, "Eyeore-like," see A.A. Milne. *The Complete Tales of Winnie the Pooh,* Dutton, 1996.

22. 14-15, "decks his dream / with enough bright feathers," *Gatsby*, pp. 95-96.

    18-19, "Young / girl in a push-up bra," Red Hot Chili Peppers, "Scar Tissue," *Californication*. Warner, 1999. Track 3.

24. 4, "deathless song," *Gatsby*, p. 9.

    15, "ghostly heart," *Gatsby*, p.96

    32, "working on his holy ghost building," "I'm Working on a Building," Trad. spiritual.

27. 2, "'Black Crow Blues,'" by Townes Van Zandt, *In the Beginning*. See Van Zandt's version on YouTube: youtube.com/watch?v=h4-kD3xXPE8. Also see Steve Von Till's cover: youtube.com/watch?v=KUUlc0E8Dmc.

30. Pictures of the bottles, information, and advertisements for Mrs. Winslow's Soothing Syrup can be seen at: peachridgeglass.com/2013/01/mrs winslows-soothing-syrup-oooh-so-soothing/. (I have taken artistic liberty with them.)

32. 23-24, "curses the universe / and does not die," Job 2:9, *KJV*.

The following two poems never found a place in the Deadman story, but they happened nonetheless:

a.

Deadman wakes from his dream pondering
words from a character in it, the one
who said he "didn't buy the accent"
he'd been given. Well, what should one
make of that? Yes, the French, now
that he thinks about it, was atrocious,
though that's not the point. His response
in the dream was only, "Really?"
Now he realizes that carton in the dream,
stick figure in a beret, was tasking his veri
similitude, while he, the dreamer,
thought it all true. This
gives Deadman pause. He must
have known somewhere that he was dreaming,
even if the character "himself" did not.
The hollow posing dummy of a Frenchman,
then, some emissary from reality come
to spill the beans to the dream
Deadman that he was just a story
he was telling himself. His skull
hurts thinking on it. Vultures
are wheeling in circles not perfect
on all planes.   They are working
their way   ever down.

b.

Deadman thinks it time to ink a sonnet—
Not Petrarch's (no loss he feels) but Shakespeare's—
Takes out paper and puts pen upon it.
But his meter, like his walk, needs repair.
His rhymes slanting near to the horizon,
And losing count of syllables,
He starts to think this po-biz might be poison,
It's worth far o'erbalanced by its troubles.
He misses writing songs where the guitar
Can cover places where his words go lame.
Here everyone can see the warts and scars,
And if it all goes wrong know whom to blame.
Time to return to writing song lyrics.
A victory most would see as Pyrrhic.

William Sheldon lives with his family in Hutchinson, Kansas where he teaches and writes. He took his BS andMA in English from Emporia State University and an MFA inCreative Writing from Wichita State University. His poetry has been published widely in such journals as *Blue Mesa Review, Columbia, Epoch Prairie Schooner,* and *Quiddity*. He is the author of two books of poetry, *Retrieving Old Bones* (Woodley) and *Rain Comes Riding* (Mammoth) as well as a chapbook, *Into Distant Grass* (Oil Hill). *Retrieving Old Bones* was a Kansas City Star Noteworthy Book and is listed as one of the Great Plains Alliance's Great Books of the Great Plains. He plays bass for the band The Excuses.